Thank You
for your Support

[signature]

Don't Give Up—You Can Make It

REGINA P. SMITH-HANNA

Copyright © 2006 by Regina P. Smith-Hanna.

Library of Congress Control Number: 2006901227
ISBN: Hardcover   1-4257-0947-8
            Softcover   1-4257-0946-X

All rights reserved. No part of this book may be reproduced or transmitted in any form or by any means, electronic or mechanical, including photocopying, recording, or by any information storage and retrieval system, without permission in writing from the copyright owner.

This book was printed in the United States of America.

To order additional copies of this book, contact:
Xlibris Corporation
1-888-795-4274
www.Xlibris.com
Orders@Xlibris.com

Contents

Acknowledgements 9
Foreword 15

Part I

Who Are Yellow Ribbons?
("Letters")

Part II

The Days Of A Yellow Ribbon
("Entries, Poems, And Letters")

Part III

When A Soldier Comes Home

Part IV

Finding A Haven In The Midst Of A Storm
"Treasure Chest"

In Memory of
Patricia Estelle (McCray) Smith
(My mother)
I LOVE YOU!
And
Grandma Jeannette (McCray) Jenkins Bellamy
For choosing life for my mother!

(Rest in peace)

DEDICATION

I dedicate this book to
ALL service members
Who are serving this country;
To the wives, husbands,
Aunts, uncles,
Moms, dads,
Children, relatives
(Including each family inside and outside of the United States);
Who are waiting
for their soldier to return.

ACKNOWLEDGEMENTS

Special Thanks

To Lillian Higgins and her family, SFC Higgins, David Jr., Ledai and Logan. No matter what I do; they always see the gift that resides inside of me. Thank You! I really believe that God made you for me (Ha, Ha)!

Thank You Jason (my love for 13 years; my husband) for serving our family and your country. Without you taking this mission, this book would have been aborted. Thanks Babe!

- Anna—you keep me going, when I want to give up (The good thorn in my side).
- J'Anthony—your spirit humbles me and makes me think of Jesus.
- Antoneya—you are so caring and giving; when I'm down, you pick me up.
- Zion—you keep me laughing and your knowledge of God tickles me.
- Mack—you have been there through thick and thin. You are very dependable anytime and anywhere.
- Antoinette—Thank you for being whom God made you. I love you always!
- Courtney—Thanks for never giving up on family; you don't mind giving second chances just like God the father. (Co-Co thanks for everything!)
- Morgan—No matter what ventures I take, you always support me, even if you don't get paid you work like you are.
- Faith—Thank you very being one of the most responsible teens I know. You manage everything well and have lots of wisdom for your age. (I Love You Girl!!)
- Grandma Tita—Thank you for being "my grandbaby" I Love You.
- Pastor and first lady Grier, thank you for your prayers and forgiveness, even when I was in the state of rebellion.

- Davon and Sherri Gray—When I was hungry, you fed me. Thank You.
- Pastor and first lady Williams—thank you for a great foundation; for it has kept me standing all these years.
- Sister Kershell—you saved my life literally, when I thought it had ended. I believe God put you here for me (I can truly say that). I was a lost sheep. I may have died if it wasn't for your discernment and closeness with the Lord Jesus Christ. Thank you for leaving church that Wednesday to come and find me. I thank God for you.

Simply Thanks

To those who helped me when I was down:

I am a yellow ribbon and I was hurting. You guys came along, and helped more than words could ever explain: Omini, Agape Christian Academy, Tony and Shellie, John and Cindy, and Mary Kay (MK) Cosmetics, Lori who offered the MK opportunity, and Carol who helped me complete DIQ.

Simply thanks, is not good enough, but it is all I have. I need to let you all know that my heart is so glad. When I should have been homeless, because I couldn't pay my rent, Omini, you took time to listen even when I didn't have a cent. Thanks!

Mrs. Osborne & friend provided food when we had nothing (your help was life to dead bones). When I couldn't be honest with anyone you were there like a glass of cold water in the desert. You offered encouraging words and your friend (Melody) provided food and personal items when we had nothing. Thanks (I met Mrs. Osborne when my journal was almost completed)!

Agape Christian Academy (Mrs. Morrison), when I couldn't pay for the kids schooling because of what I was going through (a tough season); you understood and said come work with us and in God; we'll put our trust. Thanks (Thank you for following your DREAM)!

Agape Kidz—thank you for keeping me laughing; when I lost focus. Special thanks to the sixth grade English class of 2005: Brittany, Briana, and Donovan; Thanks for writing poems.

Tony and Shelly, thank you for your help when my husband's check was late, your family was there for me. May God give you long life and love (remember your steps are ordered), thank you!

John and Cindy, you guys are the best. John, you are the greatest distributor that I know. You and your wife keep it real and most of all, you give and never look for anything in return, thanks!

Mary Kay Cosmetics thanks, I have met lots of great people such as Lori, who introduced me to the opportunity (even when she should have given up on me). She kept calling and her persistence was wonderful. When I was in DIQ, Carol was a like family to me.

She helped me with no second thoughts. She is an awesome person to know and very patient.

I believe God planted all of you in my life, at this point in time, to be a blessing. Thank you for listening to God!

Attitude Of Gratitude

Thank you God, for all of these people you sent to me, in my time of need! It reminds me of the parable of the lost sheep. Thank you for placing them strategically in place just for me.

Last but certainly not least; this book is dedicated to my Daddy and my Mom (Step-mother). Lord, where do I start? You've been my eyes when I could not see; my touch when I didn't want to feel; my hearing when I didn't listen; my protection when I had no fear; my Savior in the middle of a storm; and you are my babysitters when I had no one else at home.

Daddy, I love you and thank you for raising me with the Love of God. Mom, even though you didn't give birth to me, you never treated me different. You loved me more than you love yourself. Thank You.

Yellow Ribbon

Fathers, brothers, sisters, mothers,
Gone in a black and foreign land.
Will they return? Will they come home?
Their spilled blood covers the desert floor and turns the dust red.
That is where their precious bodies lay.
Asleep or dead will we ever know?
To stand for their freedom,
To show them our love,
We bear a yellow ribbon, yellow shining;
Just like the sun.
As it bares our men's pride, boldness, love and courage, as our men
march into war.
When will they return? We do not know.
But in the earth and in our hearts,
Their memories will forever live.
"Oh dear God of precious hope, please bring our soldiers home!"
In your good time, will they be there,
Yet until they come home,
Their yellow ribbon, will we, forever bear!

Foreword

It gives me much pleasure and honor to write a few words of commendation about this excellent and important book. I am delighted as a father, soldier, minister, and my pleasure is intensified, by the work that the author has presented with such integrity.

Regina's heart is poured out as she expresses the emotional, psychological, financial and spiritual pains of isolation and separation during a significant emotional event! Embellished with a true desire to serve God and love his people, the author shares her experience of struggle and survival. She has always been giving and suffers because of her unselfish attitude.

In sharing her yellow ribbon journal, book, and experiences; she hopes to help many other families examine their hurt and pain, while dealing with overcoming their situations.

With such glorious anticipation, the author prepares us for an exciting, truthful look at real problems often overlooked. This book gives the reader a revealing look at real feelings, unspoken, and unchanging truth. It provides the remedy to help us bear the burden for such a time as this!

The next time you see a yellow ribbon (Support the Troops), the hope in this book should remind you to Support the Families! The yellow ribbon represents one of us, all of us; we are one—yellow ribbon!

Anthony B. Smith

Our Soldiers

Our women, our sisters, our mothers;
Our men, our brothers, our fathers;
Our sons and our daughters;
Our friends and our neighbors;
Our aunts and uncles;
Our nieces and our nephews;
Our families, and our kin;
Oh when, when will this war come to an end?
Enjoy the real story about the war!

PART I

WHO ARE YELLOW RIBBONS?
("LETTERS")

I AM A YELLOW RIBBON

Dear Honey (AKA Yellow Ribbon),

    I miss you and the kids so much! I'm trying to get used to being away. It's hard! I have to go now. I love you and will soon write again and I will call when I get a chance.

                                      I Love You,

                                      Your Soldier

Dear Babe ("My Soldier")

    I miss you so much, words can't explain. The kids and I want you home now. We are also trying to get used to you being gone and it is hard for us too. Hope you're able to call soon! But just know I will be strong as I can until you come back, I have assumed the role of a Yellow ribbon waiting to be untied by you.

                                      I Love You,

                                    A Yellow Ribbon

I AM A YELLOW RIBBON

I am that yellow ribbon until you return.
I can be the tree the ribbon is tied on.
I will stand my ground
And I shall not be moved.
I will stand tall and strong
And fight till the last match.
I can be like the knot in the yellow ribbon that is
Placed just before the bow is made
Wrapping myself around our family
Until you return home safe.
I am a wife, husband,
Father, mother,
Sister, or brother.

I AM A YELLOW RIBBON

Hi,

I am 19 years old and I joined the military because I had no other choice. I am from the worst parts in my city so I was shocked to see recruiters back around my school in such a rough neighborhood. I thought this must be for me.

Mom says it's a good opportunity to get away from this place. So, I signed up and here I am months later, in a place worse than home. What have I done?

A soldier

Hi,

I joined the military when I was 18 years old; it was a great decision back then. Here I am 20 years later. I am ready to retire and cannot.

My retirement papers were rejected. I have been extended without having a meeting and without a say.

An Angry Soldier

Hi,

I am a mother of five. My husband was reactivated on January 26, 2004. He left on February 10th. So right now I'm a single parent and it is very difficult. Everyone looks to me for everything.

Although my husband is stateside, and not in the line of fire, I will not have him back home until next year-July 2005 to be exact, that's if he doesn't get extended. I am struggling right now.

The kids and I were not included on the orders and our housing allowance is the wrong amount. We get a check here and there. His pay is jacked. First of all, he left a job making $70,000 plus a year and now he is only an E5 making less than $30,000.

Sometimes I can't even buy food or gas to get around. My lights, gas, and water have stayed on by the grace of God. My kids are growing out of their shoes and clothes. My rent has not been paid.

I can't deal with everyday living. I'm unhappy and depressed.

I am a yellow ribbon!

Hi,

I am a mother of three. One of my children is physically challenged. He is blind. The other two (twins) are five. My husband is active duty and is currently in Iraq. Sometimes I feel like I'm losing control of everything. I don't know from day to day how my husband is doing.

It is weird because the company talks to him everyday and there are times that he can't call me for days at a time. So you think the company would have the decency to call me, No! I sit and worry, sit and cry, yell at the kids out of frustration, apologize and cry some more.

Until I get fed up and call the company and ask them have they heard from him and they say, yes! He's okay. We spoke with him yesterday. I breathe hard and say thanks and hang up.

I can't watch the news anymore; my daughters "the twins" are paranoid. To tell you the truth, we are all paranoid, including my son who is blind. He is uneasy and is having a hard time sleeping. Therefore, I have a hard time sleeping. These are the days of my life.

I am a yellow ribbon!

Hi,

I'm expecting my first baby in about a month. My husband is in the Reserves and was the first to be called back. He did his time and was able to come home and that's when I got pregnant.

We were so happy, until the worst thing that could have ever happened—happened! He got called back to active duty. I was furious, angry, in a daze, and wondering how I would get through my first pregnancy without my supporter-my man. I didn't think I could make it, but here I am in my last month still by myself.

I'm not sure if he will be back in enough time. I never imagined I would have my first child without my soul mate. I am brokenhearted; the contractions are getting harder with no one to hold my hand. I will deliver. I am scared and I'm in pain, pain, and pain!

I am a yellow ribbon!

Hi,

I am a spouse who lost everything. The war has crushed our family's dreams. We had to sell our house-my home because my husband got called back to active duty. He was in the Reserves, but now he is considered Active Duty Reserves.

We have nothing left in savings due to the fact that his pay is significantly lower than his regular job! I am a stay at home mom with six kids and one on the way.

When will we have peace? When will I see him? When will they pay soldiers what they are worth?

When will we mind our business? When will love start home first and then be spread abroad? When will we help our own people first?

I am a yellow ribbon!

Hi,

I am a newly wed of one year and my spouse has been gone for six months of that time. I have no kids, just a puppy that I recently got from my parents because I felt lonely.

We just moved here, so I don't know a soul. My husband's pay is a mess. He told me to expect one amount and he got paid a different amount, a whole $1200 less.

When I talked to my husband, he said that he would try to get in contact with someone at the company. I told him good luck because I had been calling them all week.

Due to the fact of my not finding a job in my profession yet and us having such a huge wedding and an elaborate honeymoon, we are still paying out the butt!

We need my husband's whole check to make it work, but he is short again this pay period. So what can I do? Nothing! Who will support me?

I am a yellow ribbon!

Hi,

I am in the Reserves and without a blink of an eye I got called back when this mess broke out. I should have listened when my spouse told me to get out, but no.

You see I wanted to retire from the Reserves even though I would not see any retirement pay until I turn 60 years old. So here I am called from my career in to the active duty.

Get this I'm making $35,000 less. In a life threatening position with sorry pay. How will my family survive? So many bills with less pay; you figure it out.

A Broke Soldier!

Hi

    I'm a wife who just lost a baby and my husband is gone to war and wasn't able to come to me in my time of need. I have to keep going. I have a two year old and a demanding job.

    There is no time to rest, no time to cry, no time to feel anything, and my husband has no time for me. Who will come to my aid?

I am a yellow ribbon!

Hi,

    We are brother and sister and we are angry because we don't understand this war. Our brother and sister had been told they could come home, but later told that they would be extended because there was no other unit prepared to come over there.

    When will we spend time with our best friends? When will we laugh? When will we reminisce about the good old days again?

    For now we must go on without our sister, without our brother, without our soldier, without our best friend!

I am a yellow ribbon!

I AM A YELLOW RIBBON

Hi,

I'm a child undone in a big world without one of my parents. I don't understand. I throw tantrums.

I am not doing well in my head and I don't have any friends; I think. I am not sure who I am! Mom and Dad say . . .

I am a yellow ribbon.

I WILL BE A YELLOW RIBBON FOR MY SOLDIER

"I am that Yellow Ribbon until you return."
I can be like the tree the ribbon is tied on.

I will stand my ground and I shall not be moved!
I will stand tall and strong and fight until the last match.

I can be like that knot in the yellow ribbon
That is placed just before the bow is made.

Wrapping myself around our family until you return safe.
As time goes on the ribbon loses color and looks worn out.

But one thing is true it's still a yellow ribbon, can't you see!
The yellow ribbon will not be untied.
Until my soldier comes back to me!

"I am a Yellow Ribbon!"

PART II

THE DAYS OF A YELLOW RIBBON
("Entries, Poems, and Letters")

Dear Friends:

"Nobody cares!" This is a line off of the movie "Flight Plan". These words were in my head even before I saw this movie. Nobody cares our soldiers are dying and wives and children are crying.

Hey, there is a hurricane/natural disaster in my house everyday. Yes, a house that does not belong to me; I am homeless.

I sold my house with hopes to build another, but the US Army Reserves called on my man. Now, since he is in the Army Reserves, and does not have the high paying job; no one will give me a loan. There is such a pay decrease and how can we make ends meet? Does any one care?

Sometimes we have no food, lights, water, or gas. There is not enough money to go around. I don't want to hear about "finishing what we started". Let's talk about why we are paying for a battle you started!

An Angry Yellow Ribbon

BROKEN

I'm broken and there is no one, I know who can fix me.
I desire, peace, life, and the pursuit of happiness
When will this truth, come to be.

I am split into two pieces
My body is here in the desert
And my mind is with my family at home,
For I still see their faces.

I am broken, who can fix me, is there any one!

Even as I hear the guns go off and blood covers the land.
My heart begins to pound for death knocks at my door.
Right here on this desert sand.

I am broken!
I once heard of a Potter, who could fix anything,
They called him Jesus, the son.

I wonder, will I ever again, see America, the land of the free.
Where we take life for granted.
We live so carelessly.

Jesus, I wish to give my life to you.
For you are the Potter
And I am broken in two.

I AM A YELLOW RIBBON

Dear Honey (AKA Yellow Ribbon),

I'm afraid and I am scared. I am hurting and I am wondering when will this war be over. I just got here, but it feels like forever.

When will I see your face? When will I stop being afraid? When will the nightmares stop? When... On the run,

Your Soldier

Dear Sweetie (AKA My Soldier),

You are a Survivor; you can make it. You are my water when I'm in the desert.

You are the glue that holds my pieces together. You are my light in the present darkness.

You are my morning after a long hard night. You can and will survive.

I love a yellow ribbon

Dear Anyone Who Cares,

I can't sleep anymore. Bill collectors are knocking at my door. I am afraid to go home.

I've had it! I can't take it anymore! When will my husband's pay get fixed?

A Yellow Ribbon

THE DAYS OF A YELLOW RIBBON

These are the days of my life. Sometimes I get so afraid.
I'm not sure what I will do.
I am losing control,
Because, I can't control everything; that my life puts me through.
My husband has been gone for just a little while,
But I still feel alone, like a little child.

I am like a child that has been left by itself at home.
Wondering when will he call?
How long will he be gone?

It has been so long, I can't see the break of day.
Oh God, how is he? When will I hear him say,
"Hey Baby, I'm fine and everything will be okay."

Well, today was not that day.
When I woke up this morning, I had a flat.
There was no one to come to my aid.
When I called the bank, I found he did not get paid.

So here I am Lord with nothing.
Here come our four kids, just fussing.
How could this be?
Why, oh why is this happening to me?
I have no energy, and I don't want to be strong.

I had to stop, think, and remember
Everyone sees me as a Yellow Ribbon,
But I still can't help to think how all of this can be.
Oh, why is this happening to me?

SOLDIER, SOLDIER, WHERE ARE YOU?

Soldier, soldier; where are you?
With hands so warm and love that sticks tighter than glue.
I need to know, I need a clue.

Soldier, soldier; where are you?
Will you call me today? I hope, I cry and I pray.
I received your letter and have read it over and over again.

Wishing that it would make me closer to you;
My close and best friend!
Soldier, soldier I need you.
To hold me and love me,

My soldier, where are you?

Dear Babe,

I can't wait to see you again. I'm sorry that everything is such a mess. Please forgive me for leaving. I love you and everything will be fine.

I went to church last week or should I say I went to a tent where church was held. I felt peaceful. You should try joining a support group or church.

I love you!

I AM A YELLOW RIBBON

Dear Journal,

Everything was perfect! Well, not exactly perfect, but better. What is going on, why me? At one time, I could buy anything I wanted.
I could buy food without counting everything in the basket. My kids had more than just two outfits and one pair of shoes. Why me?
I don't mind giving; I know the concept of giving. Give and it shall be given back to you! I've done that; when will I reap? Why me?

WHY ME?

Why me, why me? I ask over and over again.
I know I have turned away from each and every friend.
I'm ashamed of what have become.
I find myself upset with everyone.
At one time, I could buy everything I wanted.
No worry, I could call it.
But now, I have to budget, and I am having a fit,
Hating life, yes, because of all this strife.

Why me?
With four kids, two cousins, and a husband away
It is hard when there's not enough pay.
When will God hear my cry?
Let soar, and help me fly!
I am doing my best, Can't you see?
What are you trying to do? Kill me?
Yes, I heard him reply.
I had to stop, relax, and I let out a sigh.
But, why are you trying to kill me!

Because, I want to rule in your life freely.
Your way must go, my way must be
Then you will no longer have to cry Why Me!
You will be the **Yellow Ribbon,**
I know you can be.
I heard you ask for support.
Well, I'll give you a little more; a reason for your why.
Read 2nd Corinthians 12:8-9
(The Bible New Testament)

Signed Jesus

Dear God,

I don't know what you want from me. I've done my best, I think. I guess my best is not good enough, now what!

Everything is a mess. Everything is a mess. When will he call? The kids are getting on my last nerve. Every room in this house is a mess. I can't deal with this. The kids are screaming.

Help me God, now what!

WHAT IS IT?

What is it? I've done all that I can.
I've prayed and fasted, oh man!
What do you want from me?
It's already so dark, I can't even see.
I've done everything I thought you wanted me to do.
What else will you put me through.
In your word you say
If I ask for bread you will not give me a snake.
When will I hear you say, Well done, everything's okay?
I know that you have given me bread and not a snake!
But I just feel like such a fake,
Telling people how you will bring them through
And forgive their sins.
When it seems, like I can't win!
I can't even stand the pain.
I think, now is there really anything to gain?
Is there anyone, who is listening
And cares about my every need?
Yes, I know is the answer,
Because I am set free!
And I know,
Jesus Christ is the key,
For he died and he rose
Way back on Calvary,
But today is a rough day and I need a sign.
Or is it just, that I forgot to renew my mind.
Yes, that's it!
I can also use a Life Line.

WHEN

LIFE LINE

When a Life Line is given
You must be tired of your living.
Now don't get it twisted,
Sometimes this happens to a Christian.
When we don't learn our lesson
We just stop our blessing.
Time and time again, we get upset with God
Thinking that he's the one committing fraud.
When we're the ones who have gone astray.
Simply because we don't want to obey.
This is when a Life Line comes into play.
Think, what if this happened to you today?

What if you were in the middle of the sea?
Without a life jacket or company?
Who would you call? Jesus?
That's right, go on and admit it (that's all of ya'll).
What if you were driving and another car wheeled into your lane?
You would begin to pray like you were going insane, Jesus!
Uh-huh, you know that's what you would pray.
What if a train was coming and you were stuck on the track?
You would scream, **JESUS,**
And that's a fact!
The truth of the matter is this is elaborate stuff.
But sometimes our lives really get tough,
If we can just realize
Sometimes we will need to call, pray, and scream to get energized.
Afterwards we will be just fine.
And we will see Jesus as our Life Line.
ALL OF THE TIME!

Dear Journal:

I'm afraid and sick. I am tired of all this sand and I miss my family. I missed the birth of my second child. I am ready go come home!

A soldier

Dear Honey (AKA Yellow Ribbon),

I have seen a group of people blown to pieces. I cannot get their images out of my head and on top of that; I'm missing you and the kids. I hope my pay got fixed. Pray for me Honey. I cannot sleep!

Love, Your Soldier

Honey (AKA My Soldier),

I can't imagine how you feel after seeing something like that. But just to clue you in honey I'm hurting too. I'm wondering if you're okay. I'm worrying how much you will get paid this time. I know you are trying to maintain so that the kids won't worry. It's hard! I know; I am struggling too!

Your Yellow Ribbon

DON'T GIVE UP

Don't give up now
For the battle is not yet over.
Don't give up now
For the grass is greener on the other side.
Don't give up now
You've come this far, why go back.
Stand your ground!
Finish this race.
Remember
The race is not given to the swift
Nor to the strong
But those who choose to go on.
Endure till the end.
My soldier, my friend.
Don't Give Up!

Dear Honey,

God has it all in control. You must believe that for he is God and he will do everything that's needed to prepare us for Himself. The devil may have a plan, but God is the plan maker. We can do all things through Christ Jesus!

Dear Babe (AKA Yellow Ribbon),

I got your letter and I understand what you are saying, but I feel like God no longer cares. Where is he? Don't we deserve more? I just don't get this!

Your Soldier

WHERE

Where will God have to place you?
Before you say "God I give in; I'm through".
Shall we go back to Egypt?
Where there's lots of pain and no freedom
Where the slave masters tell us when and how;
And to them you must bow;
Where you work day in and out;
There is no smiling, just a pout?
Or do you need to be in the wilderness, wondering,
Walking in a daze pondering;
Where you see the same thing over and over;
Because you won't completely serve him?
In this place there are lots of tears.
For a trip that only takes days will take you years and years.
When will you see the light?
And realize what created all this pain and strife?
When will you listen and know that God can
And stop reminiscing on Egypt's sand?
When will you stop making promises you break?
And grabbing for more than you can take?

When you stop all this doubting,
That's when you will break out shouting!
And when you open your eyes and begin to see
It is the Promise Land; Come and be free.

Beth Moore inspired this poem. One morning, at around 4:00a.m. I had just, had it. I thought I couldn't make it. I just wanted to give up. I thought, what is the use. I keep trying and keep ending up in the same place.

When I heard Beth Moore on the radio say that, "there are only three places she believed we could be". (I turned the radio up) Egypt, the Wilderness, or Canaan "Our Promise Land". I started thinking and searching, "where am I at?"

Well, I consider Egypt as a land of enslavement of our mind, body and soul unto others (such as bill collectors). I saw the Wilderness as a place of desolation.

You go on and on, maybe even thinking you are in the Promise Land, and then "boom"; there's a snag and you look around. Your man made Kingdom is shredding to pieces and you are at the same spot as before.

That's me (in the wilderness) getting frustrated and complaining with my husband gone. I'm alone with the kids and it's hard. I was already in the wilderness and then life just happens. I feel like I can't bear it. Life doesn't stop to give you a "Time Out".

One thing that Beth Moore said, that I liked is, that you can be in the Promise Land here. The reason I can see this to be true is, if I let Jesus rest, rule, and reside in my life; I will be at peace.

I stopped thinking back on how good it was in Egypt or wandering in the wilderness. I will just be at peace in my Promise Land being careful, not to slip back into Egypt, or start letting my mind wander in the Wilderness.

In these trying times, I have learned the meaning of a phrase I learned when I was younger, "Take No Thought for tomorrow." (Matthew 6:34) Just before that the words Jesus spoke still ring in my ear; "Seek ye first the Kingdom of God."

Dear Friend,

Sometimes we are backed into a corner because God wants our undivided attention. We keep ourselves so busy. We say a quick prayer on the go. Thinking that it's okay because God understands.

Yeah, I thought the same way, one time. I would say he's my Father; I'll just call him when I need him. (Now this is treading on thin ice).

One thing I found to be true, there comes a point and time where he backs us all in a corner and it hurts, I mean really hurts! We think he is trying to hurt or kill us. Yes, he holds a mirror right in your face while you are cornered. To help us change our ways to lead us closer towards our purpose.

We think it's the devil, but my friend there's a place in our being that only God can get to. Not the devil not that annoying co-worker, not the boss, and not mom or dad. Not even your husband or children. Can you believe that?

The mirror is up; God has you cornered. He is asking us piercing questions; how will you respond?

A) Egypt B) Wilderness C) Canaan (The Promise Land)

P.S. I now know the meaning of through it all I've learned to trust in Jesus. I've learned to trust in God. How long will it take you?

A Yellow Ribbon

TIME OUT

Have you been running for too long?
You need a time out.
Have you been fussing and shouting at everyone;
Thinking they have a problem?
You need a time out.

Have you been thinking, is there any reason to live
And should I take my kids with me?
You need a time out.

Have you been wondering is this marriage worth it
Or should I find someone else?
You need a time out.

Have you been playing "let's make a deal" with God
When He doesn't even play games?
You need a time out.

Have you been breaking vows?
That you've made before the Lord?
You need a time out.

Time out—a place where God has you
And wants you to stay until you open your eyes
And see yourself
And change your wicked ways!

Time out—take a moment for yourself.
Do something just for you.
A facial (Mary Kay gives them free),
Maybe going to the movies,
Joining a women's group,
Or just going in a room alone,
Sitting down, and taking a breather.

A time out awaits you!

Dear _____,

When will I be at peace, I'm trying to hold on but it is getting hard. I'm slipping day-by-day and the wrong choices have given me a life of shame. I tried so hard to repent but I still never feel forgiven. I owe so many people; I just can't seem to get my act together.

The kids are still happy they love family night and other things I try to do for them, most of all they enjoy spending time with me. I'm grateful for that, I'm just having a problem with feelings or is it emotional damage, I don't know. I'm lost and I can't find my way.

I have no place to lay my head no place to call home. Maybe I shouldn't be here maybe it will never get better. Maybe I deserve to be lost for all the wrong I've done. I'm Lost, lost, lost; doing evil things seems easy and even rewarding. Maybe I should just end my life. Or should I rob a bank, or better yet I could act like I have a gun in a public place and let the police shoot me.

The only problem is, that when I lost my mom, I vowed never to leave my kids if I could help it. I never want them to experience the pain I had to endure.

The way I am feeling now is overwhelmed with motherhood (I am a single parent right now) homework, yelling kids, no money, trying to pay bills; making ends meet with less, listening to an E8 tell my husband that he will be demoted or taken out of school if we are late again on the rent.

Where was he when I was calling for help, the last 11 months? I've made over 30 calls about my husband's pay (family separations, BAQ); but nothing!

Now he (E8) adds his one-cent, like I told him "money that was due yesterday is no good today" it doesn't hold the same value! Case and point one month my husband was due a check on the 15th he never received it on that day.

We have direct deposit; the check or money never came! The bills kept coming out. Can you tell me, how, do you tell automatic debit and quick pay on line that the US Army says my husband orders are expired, and a new set needs to be cut before a check will be issued?

Well, they finally got it straight, only for finance to say the pay cycle has passed, you will receive your money around the 22nd.
You would think they would offer to pay for the NSF fees; no, they just deposited his pay into a negative account. Thanks.

I say this; I'm tired, so tired. I wish that this plate could pass from me. I wish everything could be like it was before the toils of life and sin ruined everything.

This war has ruined lots of lives; the military is under paid. The Army as I know it, does not care about the family left behind. This is my story, for now, but God is still on his throne and he has the last say.

THE JUST SHALL LIVE BY FAITH!

(I'm justified through Christ Jesus)

I AM A YELLOW RIBBON

Dear Journal:

Does God care? When will he show up? If you love me why are you so silent? If you fix this, I promise I will...
Help me! I'm in quick sand. Do you see, hear, or care? Are you even there?!!

Dear Friend,

When I find myself, saying things like what you just read; I know that soon, I will get off track so I start confirming the obvious.
God is Alpha and Omega, God is with me whether I make my bed in heaven or hell (how awesome is that) even when I am faithless God is faithful he can't deny himself (I am thankful that he is not two faced).
I am a joint heir with Christ and I can do all things through Christ Jesus. WHO DO YOU SAY I AM? (That is God's question to you)

Dear God,

    It's me a soldier; I am so lost. My wife said that she wants to move on with her life and she doesn't see me in it. Doesn't she know I had dozens of opportunities to cheat and I haven't? I use to believe that if I was good, good stuff would happen to me, but maybe I was wrong.

LOST

"Help Me I'm Lost"!
I wonder for months
Months turning in to years
Years only feeling like days in my world
A world full with pain and sin
Sin that feels good as long as you are doing it
But then pain comes
It takes control of your life.
Life means nothing to me,
As I am still sinning and not repenting
Repenting is so hard,
When you're so deep
Deep into sin
Sin . . . . it KILLS!
Stop now before you too become
LOST!

ENTRIES

These days I have been feeling down and low.

There is no support group.

There is no one I can call on.

I haven't heard from my husband in days.

When will this madness end?

I can't even deal with everyday living.

I'm stressed, with no one; not even a close friend.

WHO

When you ship my man away.
Who will come to my aid?
When he does not get his pay,
Who will come to my aid?
When you release him,
then change your mind and make him stay,
Who will come to my aid?
When I feel suicidal, but my doctor says I'm okay,
Who will come to my aid?
When my kids can't focus and make good grades,
Who will come to my aid?
When nothing but darkness fills my day,
Who will come to my aid?
When I'm so weak, can't speak,
and all I can do is lay,
Who will come to my aid?
Will you come to my aid?
That's what I thought,
I have no one, no one I'm afraid!

But wait, just before I was about to stop,
I heard a voice say...
I have come to your aid!
Do you remember when your man was shipped away?
And a church member asked you
Did you need anything and you said I'm okay?
When he didn't get paid, your parents gave,
It was I, who sent them to your aide,
But you still complained.

Dear Honey (AKA Yellow Ribbon),

I wrote this for the kids. Can you please read it to them? "I love you guys so much."

                              Your Soldier

LITTLE ONE

Little one, little one, come let me see.
I'm your Dad, remember me.

I 'm sorry I had to leave you
For such a long time.

You are growing fast little one of mine.
I want to hold you forever
And never let you go.

But it's only a matter of time
Before you begin to say no.

Little one, I want to slow the process of growing down.
When I ran the idea by mom she didn't make a sound.

So I know, this is not possible for me to do
So I will put a circle of love
That no one shall break through
Little One, I will always cherish and love you!

Dear Honey (AKA My Soldier),

I want you here and now. When will you get a break? You have been gone for 14 months with no break.

What the heck is going on; I'm scared. I am mad and I can't deal with everyday living. Everything is a crisis. I'm sorry honey.

Please forgive me; I'm just frustrated. I should have started this letter with I love you so much. Well I got to run; call when you can. I miss you!

Your Yellow Ribbon

I MISS YOU

I miss you so much
When will I see you?
Honey there's no one I can really trust
I miss you more and more everyday
When will I be with you?
I pray that you call today!

Dear Friend,

Sometimes we are so busy. We forget to take time for our family and friends. Don't get so busy that when something happens, you will wish you had more time. Put a circle around them.

THE CIRCLE

No one knows where the circle begins or ends.
So put a circle of love around your family and your friends.

Always let them know how you really feel!
Put a circle of protection around them.
Look for gaps and breaks.

Find them, find them all and begin to seal.
For tomorrow may never come and today may never end.
Use every minute, every second,
And show them how much you really care.

When your circle loses a loved one
And believe me, this day will surely come;
There will be tears, but no regrets.

No wishing you had or breaking a sweat.
You will merely tighten your circle
And think back on all the memories of so much fun.

Remembering the circle can never be undone!

DAY ONE

My Child,

How long will it take before you come home heartily to me? Stop creating business so you only have a short time to talk to me.

How long will it take, before you see that you are creating a man-made temple that will surely fall? How long will you shun away from all the people I've placed in your life.

How long must pain be inflicted on you before you accept your purpose and walk in your calling. How long, how long will it take before you really know what seek me really means!

DAY 1483

My Father,

I finally got it, seek ye first the kingdom of heaven and all other things shall be added. I know now I got it. I need to stop seeking what's at your table, stop seeking only what you can give me.

Start seeking you Jesus for my purpose then walk in my calling. Then my gift will make room for me and bring me before Great Men.

THANK YOU GOD FOR YOUR PATIENCE!

"Seek ye first the kingdom of heaven and all these things shall be added."

> Watch your thoughts for they become words.
> Choose your words for they become actions.
> Understand your actions for they become habits.
> Study your habits for they become character.
> Develop your character for it becomes your destiny.

Author Unknown

PART III

WHEN A SOLDIER COMES HOME

I AM A YELLOW RIBBON

Dear Honey (AKA Yellow Ribbon),

   I will be coming home in one month. I cannot wait. I will exhale once I see your face.

I love you,

Your Soldier

Dear Baby (AKA Soldier),

   I got your letter. Boy, I cannot wait to see you. It's been so long and I am happy it's over finally over for our family.

   You will come back home and return back to your regular job. I am excited. Maybe we can get a house now.

   Sorry for going on and on, I can't help it. I can't wait.

I love you,

Your Yellow Ribbon

TOGETHER AGAIN

Soon and very soon, we will be together again;
Like a melody and a tune,
We will be like white on rice.
Together again, inseparable,
And like a hockey player with his stick on ice.
I can feel your touch; like the hot sun on my face.
Together again; we will embrace.
I miss you so much!

NIGHTMARES

I can't open my eyes, he shouts!
Where am I; back in the war?
Please don't leave me, he cries out!
It's so dark and I'm afraid.
I can't breathe; but I must be brave.
Is that smoke?
Yes it is. There was a blast.
When I looked down I started to choke.
My legs, my legs, my arms, my arms, am I dead?
No, no you are alive and fine, my wife says!

Dear Journal,

My soldier has been home for some time now and he is still having terror attacks and nightmares. The doctors say it will stop soon, but it hasn't. Terror attacks happen when you are wide-awake. It looks like you're in a daze and a nightmare is—well self explanatory. I will tell you that my nightmare is watching my husband go through this.

WHEN A SOLDIER COMES HOME INJURED

Dear Journal,
   Today I received a call stating that there was an accident but my husband is alive and will be home soon. Lord what do I tell the kids, when I didn't even get that much information from his unit when they called I was in shock, boy I wish they would call back I have so many questions.

A YELLOW RIBBON

WHY?

Why is my soldier in a wheel chair?
What happened over there?
Why does my soldier look like all hope is gone?
Like there is nothing left; not even the Father on his throne!
What is going on in his head?
Why won't he open up to me?
It's almost as if I am dead.
Why doesn't he feel any more?
It was supposed to be such a short tour then he would come back home and everything would be back on track.
Why doesn't the news report this?
Not just the twenty thousand
Let's talk about the real list!
What about the ones who are burnt all over
What kind of life will they have?
How about the ones who stay drunk,
because they can't bear it when they are sober
What about the ones who come back and then die
What about the families
And those who have committed suicide
No, they do not want this to leak out.
Why, Why, I must shout!
Ask yourself, what is this war really about!

I AM A YELLOW RIBBON

Dear Honey (AKA Yellow Ribbon),

    I am coming home, as soon as the bleeding stops. I miss you and the kids so much, but I am afraid to come home, so so afraid to come home.
    I am not returning like I left and I feel I will only be a burden. Sometimes I feel like I am at war with myself. I feel like I should have died in the blast.
    What will I do now? How will I support our family?

A Lost Soldier

Dear Soldier,

    I love you no matter what your condition. I wish you were here so I could hold you. I love you like God loves us, unconditionally!
    I am willing to give my life for you, hold on! For better or worse; you are mine!

With Love,
Your Yellow Ribbon

Dear Honey,

    I am coming home, my stump has gone down and the bleeding has stopped. I got your letter and it was just what I need.
    I miss you and the kids so much, but I am still somewhat afraid to come home. Pray for me.

Love Your Soldier

Dear God,

    Please help me so the love of Christ will shine through me. Help me to take care of my husband when he returns I know you will not put too much on me and I can bear whatever comes my way. Father help me walk in the fruit of the spirit everyday.

FOR BETTER OR WORSE

For better or worse,
What does this phrase really mean?
I will tell you.
Honey, it means we are an unbreakable team.
We are a match and in case you didn't know;
I will not throw you back for a better catch.
You are the one for me!
My King and My Lord don't you to see
It is for better or worse.
In sickness and in good health;
For richer or poor;
I am your help meet,
And together we will soar!

WHEN A SOLDIER IS DESTINED NEVER TO RETURN HOME AGAIN

Dear Journal,

   I have 6 months left and I will be home, I hope I make it. I'm not sleeping much. I think I'm depressed. My friends have invited me to a tent service, I think I will go.

Signed A Soldier

I'M AFRAID

I'm afraid of Death.
Will I leave this place alive?
How will I get out of this Army tribe?
I'm afraid of Death.
I hide but death seeks me.
I am told to be all that I can be.
I am afraid of Death.
It knocks so very loud.
I am balled up in a corner.
I have reverted back to a child.
I'm afraid of Death.
Will some one hold me tight?
Lord God, help me fight the good fight.
I'm afraid of Death.
Why are we fighting a war that can't be won?
Well got to go I can't write and hold my gun.
A Soldier

Dear Friends

Check out the e-mail from my soldier it is wonderful.

Dear Honey,

I figured out one of my problems. I have been more interested in what the father has to offer me than who he is. He wants a relationship!

A Soldier

WHEN... DEATH!

Hi,

I'm a wife who will never see her husband again. I'm overwhelmed and I'm losing my mind.

Hi,

I'm a husband and my wife came home in a box. I'm angry and I'm Mr. Mom.

Hi,

I'm mom; I'm dad, and a parent who should never have to bury their child first. It is painful!

Hi,

I'm a sister and I'm a brother and I will never see the best friend I ever had again. I'm hurting and I'm out of control!

Hi,

I'm a child and I don't understand any of this. I want to wakeup now!

Hi,

I am the writer. I can identify with you all. I'm overwhelmed, losing my mind, and angry. A parent should not have to bury their child first.

I'm hurting, out of control, and I don't understand. This is life.

Unfortunately, we live in a fallen world and death happens; it is hard to go!

One thing that has helped me: I found a Haven! This is a place to keep me busy and happy. I am not thinking of my problems, but helping others with theirs.

Dear Friend,

He is gone! (Tuesday)

All I got is a Flag and a $400,000 policy to replace him. (Sunday)

(The day of the funeral)

That is not even enough to purchase a house. It will never replace my husband, my best friend. You know, the Army has given me "X" amount of days to move off post.

But there is no rush, they say, but I still have so many days to move. This war has torn my family apart. When will it End?

One thing's true, when you owe the government, they do not hesitate to take it; no matter what state you're in!! But when they owe you; they take forever, a year and a day! Now what?

HE IS GONE!

GONE

My soldier is gone
Now is God still on his throne?
How could he let this happen to me?
I don't understand you see?
I need my soldier to be right by my side.
He is my lover, my life, my head, and my guide.

Now here comes my friend,
She tells me to stay strong, for this is not the end.
I looked at her and all I can do is cry.

How could he, I don't understand why!
I know, you don't understand why
But maybe, I can help give me a chance, let me try.
Listen, we live in a fallen world
One filled with pain and strife.
But one day this will be over
Because of our Savior Jesus Christ.

He died, you know, many years ago.
So that we may live;
But then we must go.
No one can live forever, unfortunately.

Thank God, for Jesus who gives life,
More abundantly!
Life after death, that's what I call it.
But when we lose a loved one, we often forget.

Because of the pain we feel,
It seems as if we can't deal,
It hurts so badly.

Being human, we have to blame someone
So at God we become mad.
But for now this is just how we feel.
But God is waiting to help us deal.

Will you put your feelings aside?
Let him heal you?
Let him be your guide.

He wants to show you a Haven;
A place where you can go.
Then you will see,
Yes, God is still, on his throne.
Even though sometimes we must mourn.

LET GOD SHOW YOU
YOUR HAVEN PLACE.

WHO WILL SUPPORT ME?

"A YELLOW RIBBON"

Who will support me?
When I've had all that I can take.
When I get tired of being so fake.
Who will support me?
And tell me to stand tall.
Even when I get up, and still fall,
Who will support me?
When I've given my very last.
When I feel like I been on a 40-day long fast,
Who will support me and tell me to be strong,
Let me know trouble won't last long,
Who will support me?
When I get all so tired! And want to give up.
When I feel like there's no one I can really trust.
Who will support me and say keep your pace
Quit your complaining and finish the race!
Who-Will-Support-Me, A Yellow Ribbon?
I just lost my closest friend and don't feel like livin'.
My soldier, I'll never see him again.
WHO WILL SUPPORT ME!
I feel like my world has come to an end!
WHO WILL SUPPORT ME!
There's a pause.
There's an answer, I didn't expect.
I will support you! Let me show you.
You reach out, and I'll reach in
I'm the man who sticks closer than any friend.

YOU REACH OUT; I'LL REACH IN

"You know me; I'm the one who sticks closer than a friend."
I know you are hurting and don't understand why.
Come here; reach out and let me hold you. No don't cry.
When you hurt, I hurt too.

Listen closely, here's what I want you to do.
See me in the trees; standing strong by your side.
See me in your navigational system;
Know that I want to be your guide.

See me in the wind; I will blow peace if you let me in.
See me in a plastic bag; I want to hold your item that has a priceless tag.

See me in the winter, I want to wash you white as snow and be your mentor.

See me in the spring, I want to rule—let me be your King!
See me in the summer; I want my word to be too hot so you won't want to
    stay in the same spot.

See me in the fall; I want to change your leaves;
Just like I did for Paul.
See me in everything that you do.

I'm the only one who can help you through.
Come on, you reach out then
I will reach in and watch how your healing will begin.
I love you; I died for your every sin.

Dear God,

    It's me_____. I'm still hurting, but I must keep going. My soldier would have wanted that.
    I just wanted to share my last letter. He died before it reached him. I'm thankful he met you.

Dear Honey (AKA My soldier),

    You know I don't like writing letters much. Since your last letters, I have been touched or should I say intrigued about your finding a Savior in such a dark place in the middle of a war. Why now? Of all the odd times, I thought; but now I know why; because I found Jesus too.

THE GATE

My air is closing in
My light has turned dark
I see tear drops from my kin
The gatekeeper will be looking for the mark
Am I still lost?
I accepted Jesus, but I'm still not sure
Have I paid the cost?
Did I do my every chore?
No time to think
Dirt is being tossed
I'm moving; I'm beginning to sink
In eternity, who will be my boss?
Is this really the end?
Can I go back
To tell my family and friends
How sorry, I am for being so slack?
What will be my fate?
I am out of time
I am at the gate
I am scared out of mind.

(Don't be caught off guard, the choice is yours)

PART IV

FINDING A HAVEN
IN THE MIDST OF A STORM

"TREASURE CHEST"

MY AMERICAN SONG

America, America what the heck!
We are a very powerful country but no one shows respect.
America, America, what's going on?
We're about to go to war in the early morn.
America, America, the great and the brave!
Yet we still have war and we still have slaves.
When will we see the light of morning?
In Iraq the blood of many soldiers is yet still pouring.
I love America; you know I do.
Let's represent the red, white, and blue!
America, America hand in hand; divided we fall united we stand.
Heart to heart we love this land.
For what it's worth America will always be our homeland!

Faith

Dear Journal,

I found that when we go through things in our lives, a lot of times it's not even for us; it's for someone else. To help others with their problems, we must go through things and depending how we handle our problems will determine, if we will be able to help or hurt people around us.

If we embrace our cross and not go into isolation, not become bitter; then we will find our treasure chest and help others find theirs.

BITTERSWEET

I'm disappointed a lot.
There is a funny taste in the mouth, kind of tart.
I can't figure out how to get rid of it.
I've tried, it's sour; even my spit.
I call myself Mar'a; bitter.
I have had so many misfortunes.
It feels as if I'm being tortured.
What could I have done differently?
Is there anything?
Man, with this taste in my mouth;
I can't even sing!
The lovely tunes I once sang in my head;
The ones that keep me going; this is horrible;
I might as well be dead.
I feel my spirit pulling away from my soul.
I don't like being bitter and cold.
It feels like it's the only way to be;
For it helps me get through my day.
Is there anything that can be done for me?
Can my heart be turned from stone?
Can I get out of the hating zone?
I wonder, if I just changed my attitude towards the king;
I could change my attitude in everything.
Well, I've met the redeemer, the one who will and can restore.
For him I have reopened my door;
And I am sweet, and free as can be.
Call me, call me, Naomi
(Don't go into isolation, be free; be Naomi).

ISOLATION

I am in isolation and don't want to be bothered.
I'm sitting here pouting.
Cause I'm angry with the Father.
I am in isolation and won't help a soul.
I'm not going to move!
I won't do as I'm told.
I am in isolation, move can't you see!
I'm going to be mean.
To everyone who passes me.
I am in isolation; I think God thinks I can be molded
Don't take that away!

See, I hate being scolded.
I am in isolation come and join me.
I'm misery,
And want to have company!
I am in isolation; I don't like it one bit
Uh, maybe I need to grow up.
Surrender, and quit throwing fits.
I am in isolation, because God sees something in me
Now it's clicking!
He wants me to be the best that I can be!
I am in isolation because I wouldn't accept my calling.
I just keep running, but I also keep falling.

I was in isolation, but not anymore
It's time to heighten my horizon.
Get in the game and raise THE SCORE.

P.S. I am a Yellow Ribbon who just wants a little more!

SURRENDER

Will you give up your Isaac, your promise that God gave you?
Will you trust God enough to look at him and not
What you're going through?
Will you say God will provide;
Even when nothing seems to coincide?
Will you look at the one who blesses and not the blessing?
Will you surrender it to the King?
Will you surrender, everything?

AREN'T YOU TIRED?

Aren't you tired of living just to live?
Looking for something; but not sure what;
Because you thought you had it all.
Sounds familiar.

Read Finding Jesus on the next page.
Read it once; then read it again.

Find yourself in it and then pray;
Then read Romans 3:16-18
(The Bible New Testament)

FINDING JESUS

I have been running for such a long time.
I'm not sure what I'm trying to find going to and fro.
I'm always wanting more,
Jumping from here to there,
Falling, hurting, and not shedding one tear;
Putting up walls, so I won't have to feel;
Building them tall, so I don't have to be real;
Wondering when I can slow down!
Thinking, maybe after the next round
Acting like I have it all.
Yielding not to the one who calls;
Saying I need nothing, nope not a thing;
Going after only the Bling, Bling!
Taking that path, I hurt many;
Not caring, because I'll gain plenty.
Guess what? I was wrong in the end.
And I wound up without near a friend.
There was a void I tried hard to fill, but couldn't;
I tried everything, I mean everything,
Even the stuff I knew I shouldn't.

The best thing that could have ever happened to me is
Seeking and Finding Jesus.
With him I didn't have to give reasons
(Reasons, why I've done so much wrong).
I said sorry and He gave me a new song;
A song I must sing to you.
It's my purpose,
The thing I was put here to do,
And if you haven't found your purpose,
Finding Jesus may be the key to it for you!

PREPARATION

Preparation can be so hard when we try to remain in charge.
Do not struggle with preparation; accept it.
It is God's way of preparing you for your cross.

"Blessed is the man whom God corrects;
So do not despise the discipline of the Almighty.
For he wounds, but he also binds up;
He injures; but his hand also heals".
(Job 5:17-18).

I LOVE THE LORD

I love the Lord for he heard my cry.
He heard my cry and every moan.
I love the Lord for he died for me on the cross.
For me he was bruised, broken, and scorned.
I love the Lord for he first loved me;
And in return I will love Him, wholeheartedly.

ONE DAY

One day I was having a rough day.
Contemplating if I could deal with my circumstances;
I was down.
My good friend, an evangelist told me,
If you rebuke it and it doesn't go;
Maybe God has you just where you need to be to grow!

WORDS OF WISDOM

Don't give up on your dream!
Think of it as a baby.
Sometimes you must hold it and feed it;
Until it grows and is strong enough to stand on its own.

FINDING A HAVEN IS EASY;
DON'T MAKE IT COMPLICATED.
FIND SOMETHING YOU LOVE TO DO
AND PURSUE IT.

HAVEN

Find a place to pass your time
If you don't you will become unkind
In other words stop thinking of your problems
They weigh you down
And makes you old with frowns.
Find something that you love to do
And you will find that time flies for you.
Before you know it, your spouse will return
To a young vibrate person.
Practice makes permanent; so practice right
And when pity comes near, tell it to take a hike
You need to keep on moving
Just until you get your pace
Because in the beginning sometimes
You feel like quitting the race.
But you can't stop now
Trust me, find a Haven, there's one in your town,
A safe and hiding place!
I found one, it was here all of the time.
I must say that I stopped focusing on me
And there was Agape love in my Haven Place!

PLANTED, UPROOTED, AND REPLANTED

This is a little story about a Gardener who plants his people all over the land; even when they did not want to be moved.

Long, long a go I signed up with the Gardener. Now let me explain, signing up with the gardener was my choice. I could have been like so many others and stayed in the forest, but I chose to go to the gardener.

When I arrived I met the secretary. Her name was Confession. She asked me why was I here. I told her I wanted a change. I believed in the Gardener and I wanted to receive all he had to offer.

She looked at me with a great big smile, took my hands, and said congratulations. Boy, I was excited. I could hardly wait to meet everyone and start to go places. She picked up the phone and called someone named Grace.

She told Grace to add me to the list. I was so happy when Confession told me to go to the green house on the left. I ran as fast as I could to open the door. Just before opening it, I read the sign and it said, "training". I swung the door open and away I went.

There were stations set up everywhere. I could hardly see where it ended. Every station was labeled with a title. Soon a shepherd came to guide me to each and every station. He taught me and told me when to move on. I thought it would take forever, but it didn't.

The shepherd said because I was so willing and open hearted, it was easy. So, he handed me the book—you know "The Good Book".
I opened it up and to my surprise it was signed the Gardener, Emmanuel, and the Comforter. Each of them had written something different to me!

The Gardener wrote "I will plant you wherever you're needed, so be ready when I come; no man knows the time but me, so don't get caught sleeping". Emmanuel wrote, "I come that you might have life and have it abundantly" and "don't get comfortable where you are, you can be moved at anytime".

Now what the Comforter wrote was confusing to me. He said, "let's go", and before I could finish saying let's go, I had been zapped and planted in a place that I thought I knew, but I saw things so differently now! I could hear the voice of the Comforter.

He was letting me know things that I couldn't see or know before. I was moving so fast from green house to green house telling everyone what happened to me. I told them that I had been set free and how they too could be and live more abundantly.

Soon, humph I started to slow down. I got comfortable and even though I could barely hear the Comforter's voice, I still told the people about the Gardener and Emmanuel (when I wasn't asleep).

I acted like nothing was wrong until one day I was uprooted, snatched up from my comfort zone by none other than the Gardener and Emmanuel. Now the Comforter was still with me, right by my side. I was still afraid; I thought I had died. They asked me did I remember what was written in my book. I said, "I think so." But I did not have to think for long because the Comforter had it. You know, the Good Book.

The Comforter dusted it off and handed it to me. I was ashamed. Before I began to read, I said, I'm sorry. The Gardener said, "Uproot". Emmanuel said, "Replant", and before I knew it, I was at another green house.

I had been given a second chance. I was so happy but I wondered why they didn't put me back where I was. I did not want to start over (I don't want to be here). I started murmuring and complaining.

The Comforter shut me up and led me in and here is where my story really begins, here at Green House Agape (it was not what I expected by the name)!

I entered in and found that everyone was not the same. There were door holders. One whom I will never forget; she was so humble; had the love of God; and she was all set.

There were hall monitors. Some looked happy and some did not. Oh, let me back up, I almost forgot the three doors. Now let me tell you who was behind each door. This may send you laughing to the floor. At door #1 sat a wise woman named Whippy. She found everything I needed right quick and in a jiffy.

At door #2, you would never guess she fixed everything that was a mess. Her name was Humor. Now as I approached the very last door, I felt like I grew a little more. I stared at door #3, knocked, and there was Mercy.
Now God had placed Mercy in charge. That's why I was sent so she could lead me. As she led me to the ramp, I looked to my right and there were two champs.

Temperance and Boldness is what they were called. I chatted a little and walked away feeling tall. As we walked, I found Mercy was loving, but firm. Now something said to me here's your chance to turn. I rebuke that thought and kept right on walking because I could here the Comforter also talking.

Now don't get me wrong, what Mercy was saying would be a challenge, but the Comforter said, "Let it enhance your talent". You know I had buried my talent for so long. I wasn't happy so I decided to stop doing wrong.

Finally, we reached the top. It was a huge room filled with kids. I was in awe. There were so many kids playing, laughing, singing, and having so much fun.

Just seeing them enlightened my heart; almost as much as the Son. Mercy told me to give her a minute and she would be right back. She had to make sure everything was still in tack. As she was walking away, I saw a woman coming my way.

She had a great big smile on her face. She said, "Hi, I'm Consistency, I will help you keep your pace. Whenever you feel like you can't finish this race come and see me.
On Tuesdays and Thursdays after I've sought God's face, I will give you a new Word (Just a little taste from Heaven; right from this throne).

Immediately, I felt a burning down in my bones. My spirit lept and I thought I should cut a step, just when Consistency turned to leave! I felt a tap on my shoulder. It was Trinity.

Trinity knows a lot about God the Father, God the Son, and God the Holy Spirit. She even told me I would write what you are now reading. She gave me a big hug and told me, "this place needs your love, so hang in there. When the going gets tough, even when your flesh says I don't have to take this stuff."

Around this time, Mercy came back and said, "Alright let's get back on track. Where were we, she asked me?" I think we were going to see, "oh yeah," I said. Then Mercy said to me, "to see whom you will be working with this year." She is wonderful and absolutely tremendous.

There is Mrs. Adventurous. We bonded quickly. I'll see you later, Mercy responded. As we went in the classroom, I automatically started to assume that everything was perfect in her life, but as we talked, I found out that she was human too and also felt strife.

It's amazing how we make judgments off of only what we can see.
Well let me get back to what Adventurous showed me. She showed me how to be calm in the midst of a storm, even when the heat gets a little warm.

She also had a way with words. She made sure you understood and heard everything she had to say. She is the one who helped me with the title of the book you hold today. Now there is only one more thing. Mrs. Adventurous is A-okay.

As the day went on, I met so many kids who made me laugh and smile and so many parents who didn't mind going the extra mile. The extra mile was for their children to have things they (parents) never had or did.

There was one parent who made my day. She had nothing but nice things to say. She even had the same amount of kids as me (four). Her name is Destiny. Destiny didn't think she was all that cool, but I heard the Gardener say, she's a mighty tool.

The Gardener could use those who are humble, not the prideful, because they will soon stumble. I am so happy God sent me here (to Agape). When I was about to shout this out of the top of my lungs, I met Mrs. Over-comer.

She tells it like it is and has a strong love for her kids. She is very giving, God fearing, and living. She helped me in the time of need. I hope she knows that she planted a good seed; one that will grow from now to eternity.

When you see someone with a struggle, go and help them on the double. Here is a secret. We are planted here for each other.

Now as the day drew closer to the end, my heart was filled because I had met so many new friends (some that I didn't get to mention in this story). I know if they continue to pay attention to the Gardener, I will see them in glory.

Thank you God for Agape. You inspired me to write this story.

Dear Journal,

When I stop focusing on me, my problems; I found there were people waiting on me. I'm so glad I was able to work at Agape School. I met lots of great children and parents.

AGAPE KIDZ

YOU NEVER KNOW WHO YOU WILL INFLUENCE WHEN YOU STOP THROWING A PITY PARTY AND FIND YOUR HAVEN.

(Help someone find and open his or her treasure chest)

YELLOW RIBBONS

Yellow ribbons through the halls
Yellow ribbons on the walls
On the roof and on the lawn
On the hay and in the barn
They are upstairs, downstairs
On the tables and the chairs
Yellow ribbons in my hair
Yellow ribbons on my bear
On the car and in the car
Very close and very far
On my bed and in my head
Yellow ribbons turning red!
Color, doesn't really matter!
But still ribbons are everywhere!

WHY

Why must we have these wars?
Flags on all the doors and
Yellow ribbons on our car.
Friends and family very far
Being injured or dying
Everyone mourning and crying
No one is very proud
Of guns blasting very loud
Citizens are complaining
Fighting and arguing
Nobody is parting
People should not kill for a living
We should be joyous and giving.

FAMILY TREE

This is our family tree,
Yet it is weakening without you.
It is hard to keep on going and being prepared.
Although our leaves are breaking
And our tree horribly shaken.
We must stay on task.
For you have gone away,
And now for you we build back up.
We will never fade away
For even though our tree is broken without you.
Its very weak but we will build it stronger.
You will help us forever
And maybe longer.
For with God and your memory combined
We will heal over the course of time.
We will make it through this day
You help us build stronger
And preserve much longer
For sometimes it's hard to keep it together,
But we'll just have to surrender, and remember.

God's love will never wither.
He will never put us through an unbearable task.
For sometimes they're just challenges,
To see if we'll stay strong and last.
So, our tree is still growing tall
And our apples are very sweet and happy.
Not bitter or rotten
And now God and the memory of you will help us stay together,
For we are the family tree now and forever.

ONE DAY MY SOLDIER WILL COME BACK

It all started one day when I got married,
At age twenty-seven, to a soldier named Willie Joe.
We had a happy life, twins, and a roof over our heads,
And a very supportive family support system
To help us along the way.
Everything was going well until my husband got word that he would
have to go to war in Iraq.
At first, I thought they wouldn't take him because he was a new soldier
who just graduated from the Army academy a year ago.
His lieutenant said that he will call him back in a week to finalize
whether he would be going over to Iraq or staying home with the family
(this is what I wanted).
My husband was pretty sure that he would have to go over, but the final
decision was yet to be made. A week passed and unfortunately, he had
to go over to Iraq for a while.
On my birthday, August 22,
My husband had to leave for the desert.
Children, my family and I were very sad the day he had to go.
It had been a while since my husband left.

I had been struggling with the kids,
Trying to work,
And make enough money to keep a roof over our heads,
And clothes on our backs.
My husband was the one who brought home most of the money.
I thought I could not do it anymore,
But with God's help,
Reading the Bible, and understanding
The word, I could make it through.
The past couple of months,
I had been doing fairly well,
But not the best I could do.
A couple of months after my husband left,
I received my first letter from him.

Dear Honey (AKA Yellow Ribbon)

I have been missing you ever since the day I left. How are things going on back at the house? This is my email address that the Lieutenant gave me: *willie-joe@army.mil*.

I have some good news. I might be coming home in a couple of months or I will be over here another year. I really want to come home. It has been so hot over here with no air conditioning.

It has been really hard over here, but I am going to make it through until the end. Hold up and stay strong while I am gone.

Sincerely,
Your Husband Willie Joe

That letter had been hurting to me.
My husband might have to stay over there for a year,
But if that was what God wanted;
Then let his will be done.
I had to call my family to come help me with the kids.
Ever since the family came,
I have been doing excellent.
A couple of months had passed and still no sign.
It had been a year with no word from him;
I thought he was dead.
The month came.
It was my birthday again and guess what?
He came home.
With God's help I made it through that whole entire year.
This shows how God can help you along the way.

DON'T GO

Dear Father, don't go.
For I have just gotten here.
Shooting guns, oh no!
Seeing you go will just bring me fear.

Growing up won't be any fun.
Even when I play and run.
For you won't be there.
So I just suffer
And I am forced to bear.

Each day I pray
For your coming home day.
Dear Father don't fight and chase.
Again I may never see your face!

I want you to stay with me.
A happy family we will be.
Each and every day
Together we will always stay.

WHEN MY FATHER...

When my father went away, I had lots of tears.
My father went away.
Will he come back or will he stay?
It's like a dream.
I will never wake up it seems.
I had a wish about my dad and it came true.
I had a kiss from my dad,
He came back and I'm so glad.

Antoneya

I AM A YELLOW RIBBON

Dear Friends and Journal,

I would like to end by saying, my husband came home and everything went back to normal. But I cannot.

Shortly after my husband came home, he went to his second reserve drill and (about two months of being home) he received orders to go to Bosnia for 18 months.

So the story goes on and after I have done all that I can. I must still stand! Remember friend be not weary in well doing; you will reap, if you faint not.

So just make a decision to STAND, and after you've done all that you can, still remain standing.

God bless you
A Yellow Ribbon

Observation:

Jason is recalled to active duty for more than 18 months of training at Fort Sam Houston, TX and Fort Gordon, GA. In late August, 19 months later, Jason returned home.

During this absence; we lost our home; could not afford to buy another home because Jason's pay was cut in half (as contractor he made $70K, but in the US Army Reserves; we saw maybe an average of $1000 a month).

Our finances were depleted. We had borrowed from everyone. My father had to help us avoid bankruptcy, and for some strange reason the Army Reserves could never get the military pay correct for my soldier.

Observation:

Jason has been home for one month. He is back at work in Washington, DC and it seems that he has increased his pay dramatically.

I don't think I will have to work so early in the morning delivering newspapers to make ends meet. Things are looking up and maybe we will make it!

Observation:

After my short rejoicing, we received orders that Jason has to report to active duty. The choice he was given was to go now to Bosnia or Afghanistan; or wait until later and you will go to Iraq!

September and October, Jason is gone! The children are wondering what is going on. I could only speak to him for short periods and then a black out (no contact for about a week at times).

November, Jason shows up for the week prior to Thanksgiving, However, Thanksgiving Day 0900; he has to depart and catch his flight to Fort Hood, TX.

I am a Yellow Ribbon!

Please enjoy some of my favorite poems that I cherish

SOLDIER, SOLDIER WHERE ARE YOU...

Soldier, soldier where are you,
With hands so warm and love that sticks tighter than glue.
I need to know, I need a clue.
Soldier, soldier where are you?
Will, you call me today, I hope, I cry, and I pray.
I received your letter and have read it over and over again.
Wishing that it would make me closer to you.
My best friend,
Soldier, soldier I need you
To hold me, and love me
My soldier, where are you...?

Anna & Regina

WHO

When you ship my man away.
Who will come to my aid?
When he does not get his pay,
Who will come to my aid?
When you release him,
Then change your mind and make him stay,
Who will come to my aid?

When I feel suicidal,
But my doctor says I'm okay,
Who will come to my aid?
When my kids can't focus and make good grades,
Who will come to my aid?
When nothing but darkness fills my day,
Who will come to my aid?
When I'm so weak, can't speak, and all I can do is lay,
Who will come to my aid?

Will you come to my aid?
That's what I thought,
I have no one, no one I'm afraid!

But wait, just before I was about to stop,
I heard a voice say...
I have come to your aid!

Do you remember when your man was shipped away?
And a church member asked you did you need anything
And you said I'm okay?
When he didn't get paid, your parents came,
It was I, who sent them to your aide,
But you still complained.

(WHEN)

LIFE LINE

When a Life Line is given
You must be tired of your living.
Now don't get it twisted,

Sometimes this happens to a Christian.
When we don't learn our lesson
We just stop our blessing.

Time and time again, we get upset with God
Thinking that he's the one committing fraud.

When we're the ones who has gone astray.
Simply because we don't want to obey
This is when a Life Line comes into play.

Think, what if this happened to you today?
What if you were in the middle of the sea?
Without a life jacket or company?
WHO WOULD YOU CALL, JESUS?

That's right, go on and admit it (that's all of ya'll).
What if you were driving and another car wheeled into your lane?
You would begin to pray like you were going insane, Jesus!
Uh-huh, you know that's what you would pray.

What if a train was coming and you were stuck on the track?
You would scream,
JESUS,
And that's a fact!
The truth of the matter is this is elaborate stuff.
Sometimes our lives really get tough.

If we can just realize
Sometimes we will need to call, pray, and scream to get energized.

Afterwards we will be just fine and
We will see Jesus as our Life Line,

ALL OF THE TIME!

WHERE

Where will God have to place you?
Before you say
"God I give in; I'm through".
Shall we go back to Egypt?
Where there's lots of pain and no freedom
Where the slave masters tell us when and how;
And to them you must bow;
Where you work day in and out;
There is no smiling, just a pout?
Or do you need to be in the wilderness, wondering,
Walking in a daze pondering;
Where you see the same thing over and over;
Because you won't completely serve him?
In this place there are lots of tears.
A trip that only takes days
Will take you years and years.
When will you see the light?
And realize what created all this pain and strife?
When will you listen and know that God can
And stop reminiscing on Egypt's sand?

When will you stop making promises you break?
And grabbing for more than you can take?
When you stop all this doubting,
That's when you will break out shouting!
And when you open your eyes and begin to see
It is the Promise Land;
Come and be free.

WHY ME?

Why me, why me? I ask over and over again.
I know I have turned away from each and every friend.
I'm ashamed of what have become.
I find myself upset with everyone.

At one time, I could buy everything I wanted.
No worry, I could call it.
But now, I have to budget, and I am having a fit,
Hating life, yes, because of all this strife.

Why me?
With four kids, two cousins, and a husband away
It is hard when there's not enough pay.
When will God hear my cry?
Let soar, and help me fly!

I am doing my best, Can't you see?
What are you trying to do? Kill me?
Yes, I heard him reply.
I had to stop, relax, and I let out a sigh.
But, why are you trying to kill me!

I want to rule in your life freely.
Your way must go, my way must be
Then you will no longer have to cry Why Me!
You will be the **Yellow Ribbon,**
I know you can be.
I heard you ask for support.
Well, I'll give you a little more; a reason for your why.

Read 2nd Corinthians 12:8-9
(The Bible New Testament)
Signed Jesus

Dear Friends,

No one can fulfill your dream or your purpose, but you. During the time of this book I found that out. I tried to include people to help me with my purpose when it wasn't their passion. They have their own purpose, which they have a passion for.

What it all boils down to is that you need to fulfill your own dream. Let God lead you to it.

This journal came from the deep painful days of bucking against the brick, fighting God. I was backed into a corner so that I could see myself in the mirror.

This process began in 2004 of February when my husband went away with the military for nursing school (this is when I began to look in the mirror and stop fighting). But the previous years, I had been slipping and slipping. Praying when I felt like it, blaming my husband for everything and others. I knew I had gifts and a calling but I was running! Thank God for Jesus.

During the time my husband was away, my cousin and my four kids had a hard time, and when I thought it couldn't get any harder it did. I didn't like it because I'm human. I don't want to suffer.

I thought about ending my life but God stopped me. For I was, one throwing a temper tantrum and I was playing lets make a deal. Thinking that God would change his mind, but he didn't. He didn't want any one else but me. I have to pledge my allegiance to Lord Jesus Christ; he didn't give up on me when I deserved death, as my punishment!

I was questioning if there really was a God, because I could not get my way. I sinned just because I was angry. I deliberately went the other way (when he said go right, I went left).

Again, I have to stop and say, Thank God for Jesus, for making intercession for me and begging my pardon. Well, I have said enough, I hope that you enjoyed the book and remember, as you travel on your journey, "This to shall pass".

Seasons must change.

Regina P. Smith-Hanna